THE
Archive Photographs
SERIES

CHURCHDOWN

Chosen Hill, taken from an old print, 1701. The picture pre-dates Churchdown's Enclosure Act of 1836 so note the absence of small, hedged fields. There is also evidence of the old strip-farming pattern in the foreground.

THE
Archive Photographs
SERIES

CHURCHDOWN

Compiled by
Peter Copeland and Gwen and Brian Waters

CHALFORD

First published 1995
Copyright © Peter Copeland and Gwen and Brian Waters, 1995

The Chalford Publishing Company
St Mary's Mill, Chalford,
Stroud, Gloucestershire, GL6 8NX

ISBN 0 7524 0326 5
Typesetting and origination by
The Chalford Publishing Company
Printed in Great Britain by
Redwood Books, Trowbridge

St.Bartholomew's Church on Chosen Hill from the air. (Enlarged detail of the aerial photograph on pp 14 and 15.)

Contents

The Tea Gardens on Chosen Hill, early this century.

Introduction

Churchdown is now a very favoured residential area and with a population of over 14,000, which is still rising quite rapidly, it must be one of the largest 'villages' in the country – and a village it claims to be for it takes pride in its sense of community and cherishes its rural origins.

The parish began to grow at the end of the last century, particularly after the railway station was opened in 1874, but in 1900 there were still only about one thousand inhabitants. Once a 'bus service operated (as it did to a limited extent from 1925) and, later, when ownership of a motor car became more commonplace, Churchdown's convenient situation between the two neighbouring towns of Gloucester and Cheltenham made it an increasingly popular place in which to live. Its position beneath Chosen Hill was an added attraction – and it was probably on the hill that the story of Churchdown began.

How early in pre-history such settlement took place we do not know but a fortified encampment existed before the Romans came and the people of Chosen co-existed with their highly-civilised new neighbours. They may have 'stayed put', too, when the Saxon invasions took place but, in time, they moved lower down the hill choosing to live, perhaps, where the Green or Chapel Hay are now. Here the village as we know it began to grow, becoming after the Norman Conquest the centre of a barony owned by the archbishops of York. The archbishops and other important visitors, with their many retainers, often came to the manor of Churchdown but where they stayed in the small village is a mystery for no evidence of a building large enough to provide accommodation has ever been found – at least not yet.

The monks (actually Augustinian canons) of St Oswald's Priory in Gloucester served the parish (which included Pirton, Parton and Hucclecote) in the office of priest and, it is thought, lodged in the room above the North Porch of St Bartholomew's Church; this connection with the Priory lasted until the dissolution of the religious houses by Henry VIII.

The barony, too, was broken up in the Tudor period and the manors passed into private hands but the way of life continued much as before and Churchdown remained a small rural community; even after the changes brought about by the Enclosure Act of the nineteenth century, farmwork was still the main employment of most of the local people. The appearance of the countryside was now altered, however, for the big open fields were divided into the smaller, hedged units we see today.

The great change came this century when big industry, notably Dowty-Rotol and Gloster Aircraft, came to operate in the locality and employed hundreds of workers. Churchdown took a considerable share of this influx of new residents and so the population increased dramatically, particularly in the Pirton/Parton area of the parish (where small cottage-hamlets had existed for many years).

The newcomers were quickly absorbed into the community and Churchdown today, even vastly expanded as it now is, still retains much of its essential character and insists on its independence from its two important neighbours; it is still the 'village-below-the-hill' which, long ago, in popular parlance, was called 'Chosen.'

We hope these photographs will help to revive some memories for older residents and give to those who have come to live here more recently some glimpses of life in the village as it was before they knew it.

Hucclecote Lane, looking towards Churchdown, 1968. The drive leading to Chosen Hill House, marked by white gateposts, can be seen on the left-hand side.

One
Around and About

Looking north from the slopes of Chosen Hill.

An aerial view of the village in 1961 – showing the Hucclecote and Brockworth Roads meeting at Barrow Hill (bottom right), The Green (centre left), Church Road from St Andrew's Church

to the Bat and Ball Inn, and on into Brookfield Road (centre right).

Cheltenham Road – with the Hare and Hounds Inn extreme right. Behind the horse and cart are the Victory Cottages, now the site of new houses (numbers 166-172.) Mark Dancey's Forge, with its upstairs Mission Room, is next, followed by the pair of semi-detached houses now numbered 180-182. The single-storey building at the end is where Ted Davis once made mint jelly!

The Vicarage, as seen through the trees, with the foundation work for the new St Andrew's Church in the foreground (1903).

The Sexton's Cottage. This building, which may be as old as the church, has been much altered over the centuries. It is referred to as the 'Church House' in sixteenth-century records and was 'in decaie' then.

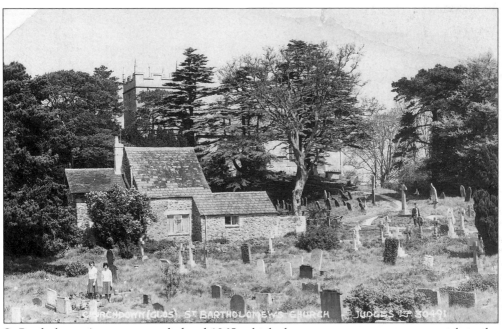

St Bartholomew's on a postcard, dated 1965, which shows many more grave memorials in the churchyard and alterations made to the Sexton's Cottage.

The Six Bells of St Bartholomew's. The heaviest, the Tenor (11 cwt. 2 qr.), is inscribed: 'H. Wright. Tobie Norris Cast Me. 1678. Blanton.' The new treble was presented in 1933 by two sisters of the Auden family (relatives of the poet W.H. Auden) in memory of their mother who lived in Churchdown.

The laying of the foundation stone of St Andrew's Church on 15 July 1903 by the Right Hon. Sir John Dorington, Bart., M.P. for the Tewkesbury Division – with some fine hats on show for the occasion!

St Andrew's Church under construction, c. 1904 – note the contractor's equipment.

St Andrew's Church, (south-west aspect), c. 1904. The pond in the foreground has since been filled in to form the site of the Church Hall.

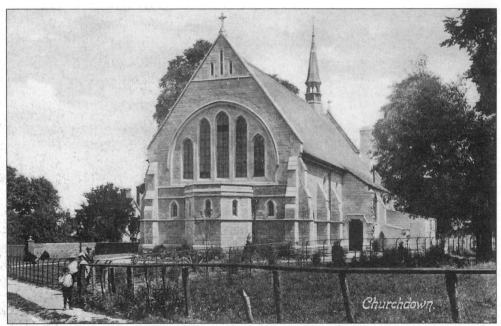

St Andrew's Church, (west end), before the War Memorial was erected in 1921.

The Choir outside St Andrew's Church, 1909. Back row (L-R) J.H. Jones, W. Apperley, J. Apperley, T. Merrett, A. Yeates, J. Garness, the Rev. J.J.D. Cooke (Vicar), E. Palmer, the Rev. H.E. Hodson, R. Merrett, F.C. Phillips, W. Swift, -?-, B. Goddard, R. Ratcliffe, W.T. Swift (Headmaster). Front Row (L-R) A. Apperley, W. Collins, H. Davis, A. Carter, P. Green, G. Smith, -?-, W. Partridge, A.C. Conway, A. Partridge.

Rogation Day Service on the 'Rogation Tump', Chosen Hill, with the Rev. C. Norton Tyzack officiating.

The Primitive Methodist Chapel, at the junction of The Piece with Sandfield Road. It was built in 1877 and services were held from this time until 1925. It became the Parish Hall about 1933 and was later used as a public library. It is now business premises.

The Methodist Church in Chapel Hay which was opened for worship in 1903. Previously the Wesleyan congregation had held services in a barn at Drews Court. (Note the original lattice-wood fencing and the trees of Drews Court orchard).

Procession at the laying of the foundation stone of the new church of St John the Evangelist on 27 April 1957. The cross-bearer is David Payne. This was the first permanent church to be built in the diocese after the Second World War.

Procession at the consecration of the Church of St John the Evangelist, 15 March 1958. The Rev. Trevor Lewis is preceding the Bishop of Gloucester, the Rt Rev. Dr W.M. Askwith.

The old brick barn of Sandycroft Farm, Cheltenham Road East, which was converted into the first church of Our Lady of Perpetual Succour.

The completed church of Our Lady after the conversion of the barn. This first church has now been demolished and replaced by a new building.

The dedication of Our Lady's Church, 6 March 1955, by Canon M.J. Roche, parish priest of St Peter's, Gloucester.

Official opening of Our Lady's Church, 19 March 1955, by the Bishop of Clifton, The Rt Rev. Joseph Ruddersham. Also in the picture are Canon M.J. Roche, Dom Dyfrig Rushton (later Abbot of Prinknash) and Miss Annie Arkell (known to many people as 'Auntie Peg'), aged 81.

Fr. Moriarty, with members of the congregation outside Our Lady's Church, 2 March 1957.

Fr. Moriarty, with young members of the congregation after their first Holy Communion, 1957. In the group are Teresa Mahoney, Sophia Zielinski, Regina Zielinski, Sheila Armitage, Mary Doyle, Sheila Lipson, Caroline Hemming, Christopher Curran, Stuart Conlon, Charles Albright, Joseph McGeogh, Sean O'Keefe, Walter Todd, Gerald O'Connor, Jeffrey Martin.

Three
Lanes and Roads

Station Road at the turn of the century. A wooden fence forms the boundary of the Village School on the left.

Station Road at its junction with The Avenue. The Chosen Hotel is in the distance.

Station Road, a few yards nearer the Station. The road was widened in 1972 and a pathway was provided on the left, changing the character of the road.

Church Road, as it became known after the building of St Andrew's Church in 1903. In the distance is Temple House, of about the same age.

Badgeworth Road (now part of Brookfield Road). Mrs J.H. Jones of Barrow Hill is seen being driven down the road in her horse-drawn carriage.

Sandfield Road, near Saroo, No. 1 The Avenue.

Brookfield Road. The house on the left, Homeside, now 46, became the first post office in the village at about the time of the opening of the station in 1874. George Preece Garness, a carpenter by trade, was the first sub-postmaster and he was followed by his widow, Anna Maria, and later by their daughter, Susannah Maria.

Pirton Lane, with War Close houses on the right, 1935(?). They were built on a field of that name.

Pirton Lane, at the railway bridge, with the Sugar Loaf houses on the right, 1938. A small inn called The Sugar Loaf stood here in the last century.

Green Lane, from its junction with Pirton Lane and Station Road, 1938. Sherwood House is centre, behind the trees.

The junction where Green Lane meets Crifty Craft Lane and goes on to The Green, 1938. The half-timbered end of one of the almshouses can be seen on the right.

Four
Farm and Farmworkers

Haymaking at Upper Pirton Farm, c. 1927. Jack Richings is on the haycart, Horace Gregory has the rake, and Bill Partridge and Ernest Davis complete the team. Jack earned £1.50 for a 55-hour week and during the haymaking season would be up at 4 a.m. and not finish until 10 o'clock at night.

Upper Pirton (Seeley's Farm), Pirton Lane, with its duckpond in the foreground. The farm has been demolished and the houses of Latymer Croft have been built on the site.

Sheep-shearing at Woodfield Farm on the Brockworth Road, c. 1910. (L-R) Harry Arkell, Martin Coopey (of Woodfield Farm), Walter Apperley (perhaps a relative of John Apperley, landlord of the Old Elm Inn), Robert Arkell, Harry Butt-Theyer (of Dean Farm) and Joe Herbert (of Upper Pirton Farm.)

Parton Court Farm in the 1890's.

Hitch's Pedigree Poultry Farm in Brookfield Road, 1933. Sid Richings (son of Jack Richings, see page 37) is on top of the cart, Fred Hunt, the foreman, is on the left, followed by Brian ?, D. Ellemore, who was serving a £20 apprenticeship, and George Clinton. At any one time there were 1,500 laying hens, and 6-8,000 chickens in the brooders.

Drews Court Farm in Chapel Hay Lane, 1964. The farm has been demolished and the modern housing of Green Lane, Crifty Craft Lane, Chapel Hay Lane and Drews Court is on the site.

The Barn of Chapel Hay Farm. This was a threshing barn of 17th-18th century type. A through draught was achieved by opening both the high doors in the picture and another pair on the opposite side. In 1885, when it was called Harris' Barn after the then owner, it was in use as a concert hall and for political and other meetings. The barn has been rebuilt and now forms part of the Sweetbriar House residential development.

Five

The Village School

The Old School House on The Green. In 1734 the Wyndowe family of the Great House (now the Manor House) provided £20 a year for a schoolmaster to live in this cottage and conduct a school there, teaching the pupils to 'read, write and cast accounts.'

The Headmaster (W.T. Swift), teachers and pupils of the Village School – an early photograph. There were sixty pupils on the school roll when it first opened in 1874.

The Village School and Headmaster's House, c. 1914, with the Headmaster (F.C. Phillips) and members of his family on the lawn outside.

The Infants' Class in 1928. the three teachers standing are F.C. Phillips, Miss Doris McKenzie and Miss Keene. Named among the pupils, and starting at the back are:- Dennis Macey, Leslie Morgan, (?), Cecil Ballinger, Bertie Mitchell, Rae Gardner, ? Baker, Joan Hill, Betty Ballard, Raymond Pratt, Kathleen Groves, Anthony McPherson, Anthony Bray, Reginald Veale, Raymond Bannister, Claude Witney, Billy Witney, Norman Griffin, Leonard Shurmer, Kathleen Mills, Joe Macey, (?), Joyce Yeates, Eric Fewster, Elsie Lowe, Gwen Davies, Nancy Bailey, Nonie Griffiths, Nancy Conway.

The School Soccer Team, 1948/9. Ken Daniell (Teacher). Back Row (L-R) Ken Stevens, Malcolm Shaw, Eddie Hurst, Michael Teague, John Hale. Front Row (L-R) Murray Briscoe, Ken Ward, Sidney Ballinger, Tony Chant, Roger Davis.

Opening of the new Village Primary School, January, 1954, by Lt Gen. Sir John Evetts.

Pupils singing to an audience of parents and friends.

The Headmaster (N.F.V. Shelley) with a group of pupils. When Mr. Shelley was appointed in 1952 there were 360 children on the school roll.

Hands up! A classroom scene in the 1950's. Note the bottles of school milk, and that all the boys are in short trousers.

The Needlework Class, also in the 1950's.

Six
Trades and Businesses

The Chosen Bakery at the corner of Chapel Hay Lane, (post 1903). This dates from about 1896 and is thought have been owned at first by Theophilus Baker, of Baker Bros. of Gloucester who ran many shops and businesses in the city. It later came into the ownership of Elias Baker, who was no relation but retained the old sign. Elias had two sisters, Popsie and Emily, who ran the Tea Rooms mentioned among the many advertisements covering the shop windows. (See page 53).

A similar scene (1904) showing the Chapel Hay Farm building on the right which was later used for a butcher's business.

The interior of the village smithy (c. 1910) at the corner of what is now called Blacksmith Lane with Francis J. Merrett, the blacksmith.

The smithy building as it appeared during its latter days with the Forge House behind. After the retirement of F.J. Merrett the business was run part-time by Daniel Cove (from Gloucester) from about 1930 to 1952.

Francis Merrett outside the smithy. His brother, Thomas, followed a different trade next door as shown by the sign: 'THOS. MERRETT – BUILDER AND DECORATOR...SANITARY WARE AND...COMPLETE UNDERTAKER'.

Alfred Scotford outside his boot repair shop in Blacksmith Lane. The previous owner of 'Ye Chosen Boot Depot' was W. Cox.

The small building used as a butcher's shop (built by G.H. Garness in 1896.) in Brookfield Road. It was later used for the storage of smoke screen apparatus during the last war and in 1952 Miss Davis opened her newspaper and sweet shop here. It has since become a greengrocery business.

The first butcher's shop in Chapel Hay Lane. It was opened in the former Chapel Hay farmhouse about 1908 by Thomas Stamp, seen here with his wife, Evelyn. On the left are Dick Pen with his delivery bicycle, and – Stoke (or Styler?) with his pony and trap; Miss Pride is extreme right. The photograph is, presumably, pre-First World War as meat rationing at the time would not have allowed such a display of meat. The business was sold to a Mr. Mason about 1920 and in 1925 was acquired by the well-known Western family.

The Post Office in Church Road, the second in the village, was built by Susannah Garness who was sub-postmistress until 1939. The premises are now a hairdresser's saloon. The cottage to the right of the Post Office was rebuilt in a matching style and later became a Co-op stores. On the extreme right is the Old Elm Cottage.

Mrs. Walker, with local children and horse 'Kit' in Innsworth Lane. She ran a door-to-door trade in greengroceries around Churchdown for many years.

The Chosen Hill Tea Gardens at Yew Tree Cottage. They were run by Mrs Berry and, later, by her daughter, Mrs Edith Fishlock, and her husband, John.

The Baker's Tea Gardens, which were on the lawn of Prospect House, on the Church Road side. (Braemar now occupies the site).

The Dancey Brothers' Petrol Station in Cheltenham Road, c. 1920's-1930's. Thomas and Edith Dancey are standing in the forecourt adjoining the old forge and Mission Room.

The delivery van of Colville, baker and grocer, The two-figure telephone number suggests a date in the middle 1930's. The driver is Leonard Franklin and the van boy is Donald Lowe.

C.H. 'Ray' Smith with his 1-ton Morris truck ready for a London to Brighton run, 1926. Mr Smith ran the 20-acre Hill View Farm in the 1920's-1950's, most of which was a fruit and vegetable holding including an orchard of 5,000 trees. The grounds of the farm covered the area from the Cheltenham Road to the R.A.F. camp at Innsworth. Snowdon Gardens now occupy part of the site, while Town Cars use Hill View, the former farmhouse, as their offices.

Ray Smith with a larger vehicle, a 3-ton Bedford truck c. 1955. Mr Smith is at the wheel with his son, Russell, behind him and Tommy Marsh at the back.

The Retreat, next door but one from the Post Office in Brookfield Road. The shop was the butcher's business of William Procter, later that of William Mitton. The premises were later used by Chris Green, a coal merchant, the cottages at the rear being then lived in by Green's daughter and son-in-law, Mary and Arthur Griffin, and also by Bert Wager and Clarence Lovesey, both postmen. The buildings were demolished in 1967 and a modern house, No. 12, has been erected on the site.

The butcher's premises of J.H. Western & Sons Limited, 1983. The Western family were the last owners and ran the family business for over sixty years.

The Rotol Factory brought industry to the Churchdown area. During the Second World War it played an important part in aircraft production by its manufacture of air screws.

Hurrans Nurseries from the air, 1959. (Briars Close is in the foreground while the St John's Avenue and Stansby Crescent roads are laid out but with only the Church of St John the Evangelist built).

The new Hurrans Garden Centre in Cheltenham Road, 1967. This was created from the original Hurrans Nurseries and was opened at a ceremony on 12 April. Percy Thrower cut the ribbon on a pair of ornamental gates. On his right are Allan Barnett, manager, and Stewart Hurran.

Allan Barnett and Percy Thrower admire a display bed. Stewart Hurran points out a feature to the Mayor of Gloucester, Councillor A.G. Neal.

Seven

Local Inns

The Hare and Hounds Inn in Cheltenham Road. The bunting and the brass band suggest a festive occasion of some kind. The licensee's name, E.M. Romans, over the entrance, dates the scene to the 1920's-1930's.

Ye Olde House At Home, a beerhouse in Brookfield Road at the turn of the century. The doorway notice reads: 'Old House At Home. George Henry Garness, Licenced to retail Beer, Ale, Porter and Cider. To be consumed on the Premises. Dealer in Tobacco.' The premises were closed in 1913 as part of a campaign by Lloyd George to reduce drunkenness.

Ye Olde House At Home, long after closure.

The Old Elm Inn in Church Road, now demolished. It was previously known as The Elm and, before that, The Rising Sun.

The Old Elm Inn seen from Chapel Hay Lane, (pre-1938). On the right the Chosen Bakery can be seen; part of the wall of the butcher's shop is on the left.

'Ye Olde Elm', (a change of name, c. 1938.) The new Bat and Ball Inn which replaced it can be seen under construction at the rear. Licencing laws required no break in continuity of occupation (or the licence was forfeit) so the new inn could not be built on the site of the old.

Stone built into the front wall of the Bat and Ball Inn and inscribed: 'T. THACHE. 1695'. The Thache family had once held much property in the village. The stone is known to have been built into one of the chimneys of The Old Elm.

An early picture of The Bat and Ball Inn with an elm tree in the forecourt. In the background is the old blacksmith's shop.

The Bat and Ball Inn with an earlier inn sign. Note that the elm tree has been felled and the blacksmith's shop demolished.

A modern picture of the Chosen Hotel by the station, (pre-1975). It was built in 1897 and opened as a temperance hotel, a licence being refused at first. It closed in the 1990's because of lack of custom and the Priory Court development has been built on the site.

Eight
The Railway Station

Churchdown Station (between 1900-1904). The railway was constructed through the village in 1840 but a station was not provided until 2 February, 1874. In this view, from a post card card dated 1904, a Great Western Railway 'Atbara' Class 4-4-0 locomotive is seen hauling a train from Gloucester. This class of engine was not built until 1899/1900.

Outside the Station, 1910. In the picture are the Rev. H.E. Hodson and Gladys Veale, who later became Mrs Adams.

A view at platform level. A G.W.R. train, hauled by a Metro Class 2-4-0 tank engine approaches from Cheltenham. The footbridge was a late addition provided as the result of a request made by the Parish Council in 1902.

A Midland Railway train hauled by a Johnson 2-4-0 on a non-stop train heading north from Gloucester.

A through-train from Manchester to Bournemouth, pre 1927. It is hauled by a Midland Railway 4-4-0 engine, and unofficially titled 'The Bournemouth Express' on the postcard original. The through service was introduced in October, 1910, but only acquired the title of 'The Pines Express' in 1927 so the scene indicates a date prior to this.

The station in 1933. The end of the right-hand building has been remodelled with the windows filled in and a new chimney stack.

The station in 1946, showing the two additional tracks and two island platforms provided in 1942. The density of Second World War traffic made this rebuilding necessary, and also the provision of a new signal box and new administrative offices on the approach road. The left-hand platform shelter is the original building, with its roof cut back, but the other platform has completely new buildings. Porter Beatrice Scotford is meeting a local G.W.R. train. (One of the old Grotto cottages can just be seen behind the new retaining wall).

The Station Road Bridge before start of extension work, January, 1942. The road bridges at Sugar Loaf and the Station were extended to accommodate the extra tracks mentioned opposite.

Station Road Bridge, an intermediate stage of the reconstruction, May, 1942. Timber beams with corrugated iron sheet parapets provide temporary spans over the lines, and a contractor's railway runs over the site of the cleared embankment.

Station Road Bridge, July 1942, with new track in position under the new right-hand span but not yet under the left.

The station in July, 1946. It was given a new, solid-sided footbridge, which also now served as a public footway for the road bridge. Its dual nature required that the gates to the platforms were kept locked when the station was closed.

Signalman Bert Williams in the new signal box, late 1940's. Note the four-track diagram and the air raid shelter extreme left.

The Staff of the joint Midland/G.W.R. station. The stationmaster, third left, is Daniel Joseph Gilkes, who was in charge from 1884 to 1918. The left-hand figure is thought to be Albert Dobbs.

A lineside post, May, 1947. This was visible from Sugar Loaf Bridge and was a reminder that the common lines between Cheltenham and Gloucester were originally owned in separate halves by the first railway companies, the Birmingham and Gloucester (later the Midland and, still later, the London, Midland and Scottish – hence the 'L.M.S.') and the Cheltenham and Great Western Union (later the Great Western or 'G.W.R.'). Neither company could agree to the more usual arrangements under such circumstances – joint ownership – and the compromise was for each to buy their own land and build their own track. Maintenance was afterwards carried out separately, to either side of the marker post.

An accommodation underbridge, a quarter of a mile on the Cheltenham side of the station overbridge, 12 October 1940. The north portal had at one time a stone with the inscription: C AND GW UNION RAILWAY. THIS BRIDGE WAS BUILT FEBY AND MARCH 1839, a reminder of the original division of construction work on the line. The plaque was buried from sight when the bridge was extended in 1942, but can be seen, arrowed, on the left of this picture.

Nine
Village Occasions
and Activities

A Conservative Party Political Meeting, 1906. The candidate was Sir Michael Hicks-Beach, presumably one of the two bowler-hatted men in the carriage. Note the campaigning dog!

The seven-piece orchestra of the temperance Chosen Hotel, early 1900's. The musicians were mostly members of the Franklin family, Mr Franklin being the hotel owner. Musical afternoons took place on Thursdays during the summer.

The Primrose League's annual outing, 1913. Among those awaiting their train at the station are Reg Merrett, Mrs. J.H. Jones, Mrs Reg. Merrett and (facing the camera) Jim Garness.

The annual Church Parade of the Churchdown Branch of the Gloucester Conservative Benefit Society, September, 1907, outside the Old Elm Inn.

A Primrose League gathering, 1924. This was held in Hawkes' Field, next to the Village School, and among those present are: Jack Cole, Vera Wilkes (née Nicholls), Ted Woodhouse, Doris Sprague, Maud Collins, Grace Collins, Elsie Lewis, Mrs Crane, Mrs Phillips, F.C. Phillips, Miss Streatfeild-James, ? Nicholas, Ron Vizard, George Baldwin, Alec Tombs, ? Nicholas, Ethel Tombs, Irene Pitt.

Festivities to mark the Coronation of King George V and Queen Mary, 22 June 1911, included a Fancy Dress competition which attracted this group of hopefuls!

The Celebration Bonfire on Chosen Hill. This was lit at the conclusion of the day's events and was the usual finale for such occasions in Churchdown.

Children waiting to perform around the Maypole, May Day, 1922.

Sir Leslie Boyce, M.P., opens a Church Fete, 1950's. Among those present on the platform are Mrs Adams, Mrs Maud Hanks, Lady Boyce, The Rev. C. Norton Tyzack, Mr and Mrs Arthur Hurran and Mr Norman Shelley.

Volunteers at the making of the Churchdown Club's Bowling Green, 1924. Back Row (L-R) G. Morris, E. Woodhouse, F. Baldwin, G. Garness, E. Daniels, D. Gale, G. Holford. Front Row (L-R) T. Holford, A. Wager, Dr R.D. Moore, E. Hook, J. Garness, R. Merrett, F.W. Conway.

The Churchdown Pageant celebrating the Coronation of Queen Elizabeth II, 2 June 1953. This was directed by Mrs Temple Morris and held in King's Field in Parton Road. The History of Churchdown was portrayed in various scenes and this is Episode I, 'The Roman Occupation'.

The Coronation Pageant, 1953, Episode IV, 'The Granting of a Charter to Hold a Faire by the Archbishop of York'. Some of those taking part are: Frank Chinery, Jo Shearman, Peggy Chinery, Gladys Webley, Bryan Shearman, John Webley, Russell Mutlow, Betty Mutlow, Joan Bircher, Ken Bircher, Winifred Miles, Maud Hanks, Susan Chinery, Jane Mutlow, Elizabeth Warriner, Jill Davies.

Opposite: Churchdown Horticultural and Sports Society, members and officials. (L-R) (Standing) Miss Ivy Hodges, A.E. Robinson, Mrs Elizabeth Thomas, A. Mann, C. Daft, H. Lane, ? Watts (senior), Mrs.Daft, -?-, Mrs Forsyth-Williams, Mrs Houston, Mrs Henn, Mrs.Frewing. (Kneeling) MrsToomey, -?-. (Front) Miss Toomey, Miss Janet Scott-Williams, -?-, Commander Robson, -?-, Miss Molly Cockayne.

The Coronation Pageant, 1953, Episode VI, 'Guests at the Great House.' Sir Walter Raleigh is seen making a present of cigars and potatoes to his hosts.

The Churchdown Players' Production of the Pantomime *Red Riding Hood*, 1946. Back Row (L-R) Daphne Wilson, Pamela Risbey, Sheila Conway, Mrs Conway, Mrs Lane, Hubert Yeates, Mrs Danvers, Mrs Sheather, Mrs Olive. Middle Row (L-R) Mrs Lapham, Mrs Packer, Mrs Jarrett, Moira Leach, Pearl Conway, Joyce Greening, Vera Hill, Roy Packer, Iris Holden, Rita Tomkins, Len Brown, Mrs.Bray, Mrs Usher. Front Row (L-R) Margaret Adkins, Jill Crisp, Audrey Ockland, Janice Hill, Pat Hook, Barbara Packer, Pauline Hook, Morven Yeates, Margaret Risbey, Janet Ravens, ? Goodrington. The Wolf was played by Mr Usher and Bonzo the Dog by Margaret Western!

Opposite: Some of the Hunt on The Green, by Green Farm Cottage. Mrs Freeman holds the reins of Mary Western's mount; on her other side is her sister, Mrs Miles.

The Cotswold Vale Boxing Day Meet. The Master of the Hounds receives his stirrup cup at the Bat and Ball Inn.

The Langford Players' production of *Mr Pym Passes By*, 1957. (L-R) Gwen Crohill, Edward Day, Dr David Chase, The Rev. Norton Tyzack, Vera Tanner, Doris Fenton, Anne Temple Morris.

Prizewinners at the Churchdown Horticultural Show, late 1950's. (L-R) Gwen Crohill, -?-, Doris Potter, H. Pugh, Zoe Duke, Don Strange.

Harvest Supper in St Andrew's Church Hall, 1958 or 1959.

Cheltenham Road East Over-60's Club, on holiday at Ostend, September, 1964.

The Opening of Parton Road Branch Library, 23 April, 1966, by Lt Col. A.B.L. Lloyd-Baker. Also on the platform are: The Rev. L.E.G. Lewis and councillors Noel Thomas and G.J. St John Sanders.

Churchdown Women's Institute 40th Anniversary, 26 October 1965. Seen planting a commemorative tree are the President, Mrs Marjorie Goodman, and Councillor Noel Thomas.

Ten
Times of War

Churchdown says farewell, on 4 September 1914, to recruits from the village joining up after the outbreak of the First World War.

The Churchdown Home Defence Corps in 1914. Front Row (L-R) Police Constable Hayden, Samuel Bendall, Joe Champion, The Rev. J.J.D. Cooke, J.H. Jones, Dr Moore.....

Local men taking part in a post-war pageant at the 'Victory Sports', 1919.

The Chosen Hill 'Peace Bonfire', 19 July 1919.

The Unveiling of the War Memorial, outside St.Andrew's Church, 3 April 1921.

Remembrance Day Parade in Station Road, 13 November 1932. Among those on parade are, in the front row, ? Griffin, Jim Tombs, Bill Davis, Frank Shurmer, Ernie Bannister, Bill Bishop, Charlie Anderson, George Duford, Reg Merrett.

Girl Guide Parade in Station Road on Remembrance Day, 13 November 1932. (Barn Hay House is in the background). Immediately to the right of the Union Flag are Grace Collins, Lillian Bell, Maud Collins and Dorothy Shepherd.

Remembrance Day Parade in Station Road, 13 November 1932. Among those in the front row are Albert Watts, Hubert Yeates, Bill Yeates, Bill Potter and Bill Yeates (junior).

Evacuees from St.Anne's Roman Catholic School, Birmingham, 1940, having a meal following their arrival. Among the lady helpers are Mrs Elsie Thomas, Mrs Collins, Mrs Temple Morris, Mrs H.A. Lane and Mrs Len Brown.

Their Majesties King George VI and Queen Elizabeth arriving at Churchdown Station, 10 February 1940, for a visit to a local wartime factory. Colonel W.F. Henn (of Parton Grange), Chief Constable, is in the centre.

Thomas Dancey, of Cheltenham Road East, in Civil Defence uniform, 27 March 1943.

Bomb damage at Hurrans Nurseries, 10 October 1940. Apart from the damage to production, the attack also resulted in the death of Mr Albert Preston, an employee. It is thought the bombs were intended for the Rotol factory, the glass-houses perhaps giving the appearance of factory buildings.

An unexploded bomb (1000 lb) found at the nurseries after the above-mentioned attack, 10 October 1940.

Members of Churchdown Home Guard at Sneedham's Green during the early years of the Second World War. Among those identified are: Sgt Franklin, Capt. Palmer, ? Preece, Major Preece, Jack Jefferies, Henry Western, Frank Earl, George Duford, Ted Turville, Bill Edden, George Turner, J.H. Western, Jack Cecil, Geoff Newcombe, Sid Conway, Ted Smith, Sgt A. Watts and Jim Tombs.

CHURCHDOWN VILLAGE WELCOME HOME FUND

PRESENTED TO

BY THE INHABITANTS OF CHURCHDOWN VILLAGE FOR SERVICES RENDERED TO KING AND COUNTRY DURING WORLD WAR 1939 - 1945

Certificate presented, with a cheque, to the returning service men and women, 5 September 1946.

'Welcome Home Supper,' held at the United Services Club, 5 September, 1946. Among the guests on the left-hand table, left side (L-R) are: A. Mann, Mrs Winstone, Mrs Elizabeth Taylor, Mrs Mitchell, Mrs Temple Morris, R.H. Hitchings, N.J. Briscoe, R.T. Merrett, -?-, Les Smith, -?-, ? Bannister, Bob Davis, ? Morgan. Right side (L-R) Mervyn Moore, Miss Ivy Hodges, -?-, Mrs K. Duford, Mrs S. Duford, Mrs Western, Mrs Robertson, Mrs Oakey, R. Stafford.

'Welcome Home Supper,' 1946, Centre table, left side (L-R) Clifford Lovesey, Ray Lovesey, -?-, -?-, Neville Spencer, Stan Williams, G.W. King....... Right side (R-L) Miss Arkell, Mrs Spencer, Mrs Hyett, Mrs H.A.Lane, Mrs Cole, Mrs Jarrett, Mrs Henn, Mrs Hinton.........

'Welcome Home Supper', 1946, Right-hand table, left side, (R-L) -?-, Mrs Griffin, Mrs Dorothy Green, A.H. Wiggall, Alf Woodman, Mrs Mary Sleep, Ken Sleep, Ray Mitchell, Frank Conway, ? Morgan, J.H. Proctor, H. Nicholls....... Right side (R-L) Mrs Yeates, Mrs Maud Hanks, Mrs Kilminster, Mrs Shurmer, Mrs Cox, Jack Pitt, Jack Jones, -?-, -?-, A Goodbody (standing) -?-, Arthur Gregory..... Top table, J.H. Western and Henry Western.

The Rotol factory in camouflage colours, 8 May 1945. Being a prime enemy target, the factory was also protected during an air raid alert by a smoke screen from the locally-sited (and detested) 'Smokey Joes,' which were ignited canisters of oil. The decorations were for V.E. Day.

Churchdown Branch of the British Legion at Badminton, early 1950's. Back row (L-R) Albert Watts, Lou Barnes, George Turner, Tom Dobson, Frank Earl, Fred Adams, John Dancey, A. Goodbody, Mervyn Moore, -?-, ? Packer, Hubert Yeats, R.T. Merrett, Ken Sleep, Henry Duford, -?-, Dick Baker, H. Nicholls, Charlie Anderson, Ron Hughes, Fred Hanks, H. Lane, Jim Tombs, Reg Merrett. Front row (L-R) Cecil Dobson, David Dobson, Henry Morgan, -?-, Jack Matheric, J.H. Western, Bert Day, George Duford.

Remembrance Day Parade. Bat and Ball, late 1950's or early 1960's, (L-R) Henry Duford, Reg Merrett, George Duford (Standard Bearer) , R.T. Merrett, C. Anderson.

Ele en

Houses and Cottages

The Manor House, a misnomer, as the building never functioned as a manor house. It was in the possession of the Raleigh family (relatives of Sir Walter, the famous Elizabethan courtier and explorer); later it became the home of the Windowe family. The exact age of the house is unknown; it may be earlier than the 17th century, at least in foundation. It is now part of 'The Manor' residential complex.

The small cottage (demolished c. 1970) which at one time was at the rear of Ye Olde House in Sandfield Road. This ancient building was of timber-framed construction and, originally, of wattle and daub infill. Miss Ellen Smart lived here for many years and died, in 1969, at the age of 103, 'having just eaten a hearty meal'. She often stood at the gate by the road with a stick, shouting loudly at her cat.

The thatched pair of the four almshouses in Green Lane, which were demolished in 1918. These, and the other slate-roofed pair next door, were provided for the use of 'four poor old People' by the Richard Holford Charity of 1668.

The two pairs of almshouses, on the corner of Green Lane and Crifty Craft Lane.

Mulberry House on the Green, a timber-frame building with brick in-fill between the wooden studding.

The thatched, and timber-framed cottage in Pirton Lane which now forms part of the modern 'Chequers,' photograph c. 1920. The cottage belonged to Upper Pirton Farm. The three children are (L-R) Ellen Richings, her brother, Sidney, and Audrey Freeman.

Green Farm Cottage on The Green, early this century. The notice reads: REFRESHMENTS. TEA AND WATER AND MILK PROVIDED and this was one of the many places in the village at which refreshments could be obtained.

Green Farm Cottage, Churchdown.

Green Farm Cottage, a more recent view. The thatched roof has been removed, the upper storey rebuilt and the kitchen extension altered.

The row of three cottages on The Green, with the two end buildings slate roofed and the centre one thatched.

The three cottages on The Green again, on a post card dated 1956 (but the vintage car belongs to the 1930's). The three cottages were rebuilt as one house, Chosen Hay, in 1949.

104

Barn Hay, at the top end of Station Road. The house was built for Mr N.M. Wellington, owner of paper works in Southgate Street, Gloucester. The house was pulled down in 1970 and replaced by the Barn Hay group of houses.

The former Woodbine Cottage at the junction of Blacksmith Lane and Sandfield Road. It is thought to have been built about 1868. The last occupant was Miss Ellen Mary Daniels who died in 1969, aged 92. The cottage was pulled down soon afterwards.

Annandale House, in Station Road, built in 1888. It later became Caer Glow, when it was occupied by the Misses Auden, sisters of W.H. Auden, the poet. It is now Stanton House, a block of flats.

Elm Villa, in Blacksmith Lane, for many years the home of the Collins family. It has been replaced by a modern house of the same name.

The Old Elm Cottage, Church Road, occupied at one time by the Vye family, who rented a room to Dr Prance, of Cheltenham, for use as a surgery, the village then having no resident doctor. On the right, and behind, are other cottages which were later replaced by shops. The Old Elm Inn is extreme right.

Brookfield, Brookfield Road, the one-time home of Mrs Peninnah Holford, who provided TEA for many years, and who was the grandmother of the present occupant, Miss Joan Holford.

Parton Lawn, in Parton Road. The modern houses of Summerland Drive now occupy the site.

Dunstan Lodge, in Paynes Pitch. In the foreground is Mrs East, with one of the Alsation dogs she bred.

Dunstan Cottage, in Chapel Hay Lane, for many years occupied by the gardener of Dunstan Lodge. Note the repairs being carried out to the thatched roof.

Chapel Hay Lane, the narrow road as it once was. Western's butcher's shop is far left, and Melrose (No. 5), extreme right, was the post office from 1939 to 1956.

Churchdown, Glos

Brooke's Series.

Chapel Hay Lane, from Church Road, and soon after the Methodist Church was built in 1903. Next to the church are Gothic Cottages, flanked by the corner of Chapel Hay farm buildings. The sign on the left, pointing up the hill, reads 'TEA GARDENS . LUNCHEONS & TEAS PROVIDED . SODA & MILK.'

Twelve

Personalities Past and Present

A gathering on the Vicarage lawn on the occasion of the retirement of the Church Organist, Mr Sidney Cullis.

Some early inhabitants! These human remains were found in Chapel Hay field when ground for an extension to the sports facilities of the United Services Club was being excavated in 1924. The skeletons may be medieval or earlier.

The laundresses of the Wash-house on The Green, depicted, probably, at the turn of the century. The Old School House is in the background. A laundry service was provided for the households of several large houses in the locality.

Elias Baker, one-time owner of the Chosen Bakery, with his two daughters, 1915. He is in the uniform of the Royal Artillery and is thought to have served with the Divisional Field Artillery of 81 Division during the First World War.

The wedding day photograph of Thomas Stamp and Evelyn Hayden outside their first home at 1 Lypiatt Cottage, Brockworth Road, 23 October 1906. The groom was then bailiff to Mr. J.H.Jones of Barrow Hill but, later, in about 1908, he set up business as a butcher in the Chapel Hay Farm premises in Chapel Hay Lane (see page 51.)

Mrs J.H.Jones of Barrow Hill seated in her horse-drawn carriage, 1910. A cousin sits beside her and the coachman is Samuel Flaye.

The family of Mr and Mrs Daniels of the Old School House, late 1890's.

Dr. Reginald Devereux Moore, Churchdown's first resident doctor, who was in practice from 1900 to 1945. He was commissioned captain in the Royal Army Medical Corps in 1915, serving first as a medical officer with the 5th Battalion Glosters. He is seated, right, in the front row.

Dr Joseph John Foster, Churchdown's second resident doctor, seated outside Deerhurst Church in his 3½ HP Renault, registration number AD 61. This car had a two-speed gear and tiller steering and was one of the first motor cars to be seen in and about the village.

Dr Foster with George Dancey seen being trained to be the chauffeur. Dancey soon left, however, to join his father at his blacksmith's business in London Road, Gloucester, and afterwards set up his own business in Down Hatherley.

William F. Colville and assistant Mary Poole outside the Chosen Bakery in Chapel Hay Lane.

A group taken at the Station, but with no record of reason for the occasion. George Garness is third from left, back row, and Dick Holford, is second from the left front row.

Mrs Salcombe, wife of Jack Salcombe opposite. In 1924 the Entertainments Sub-Committee of the Churchdown Club granted her free admission to all entertainments as an appreciation of her splendid services as a ticket seller.

Thomas Dancey, blacksmith, and landlord of the Hare and Hounds Inn from about 1851 to 1885. The horse was used to work the cider mill.

Jack Salcombe, railway ganger, with his track gauge, and taken near the station. He lived at Brookfield Cottage, next to the greengrocer's shop.

Children on the back of the famous Fishlock donkey on Chosen Hill, 1924. Jack Dancey, aged 5, great-grandson of Thomas Dancey, is on the right. The donkey was used to bring provisions in panniers from the village up to the top of the hill.

Josiah Collins in the uniform of the Churchdown Brass Band.

The Collins family: Mrs Price, grandmother, and Alice and Josiah, parents of the baby, Frederick, outside The Elms (now The Pines), Green Lane, 1895. The Pines was one of the many tea-rooms which flourished in the village and Mrs.Collins had many a sore thumb from opening lemonade bottles for thirsty excursionists, most of whom came to Churchdown by train from Gloucester and Cheltenham. All the Collins family moved to Elm Villa in Blacksmith Lane in the 1920's.

The Collins family outside Elm Villa in Blacksmith Lane. Josiah and Alice, and, after them, their daughter, Grace, (left) were, successively, vergers of St Andrew's Church from 1926 to 1976. On the right is Grace's twin sister, Maud, who became Mrs.Hanks.

The Sports Teams of the British Legion Club, 1932. Back row (L-R) W. Luker, F. Wilson, F. Smith, F. Shurmer. Middle row (L-R) G.R. Morris, W.H.G. Harrison, W.F. Colville, J.H. Hughes, J. Tombs, R. Turner, J. Proctor, A.G.C. Watts, R. Merrett, S.J. Harrison. Front row (L-R) C.F. Anderson, H.A. Lane, (Sports Secretary), B.E. Toomey (Bowls Captain), A. Dickenson (Skittles Captain), R.A. Horlick (Billiards Captain), R. Richardson, C. Evans.

Mr John Holford, of Brookfield, Brookfield Road, an employee of the G.W.R. for many years. The name Holford occurs quite frequently in the archives of Churchdown in past centuries.

Mr Albert Holford, son of John Holford, farmed on Chosen Hill for many years.

Mr C. Streatfeild-James, of Parton Grange. He was an active member of the Church and, at various times, was Church Warden, Hon.Treasurer of the Parochial Church Council and Secretary and Treasurer of the War Savings Committee set up in 1916. He conducted the evening services in the Cheltenham Road Mission and, with the Rev. A.P. Willway, started the Free Will Offering Scheme in 1921.

Mr Alfred Hurran. He had long-established horticultural businesses in Gloucester and bought the Churchdown Fruit and Flower Company's Nurseries in Cheltenham Road in 1928.

123

Mr J.H. Western, owner of the Churchdown butchers business, outside his home in Chapel Hay Lane.

Members of the Western family gathered outside 'Chapel Hay'. In the photograph are (L-R) Mervyn, Mary, Margaret, Anne (wife of Kenneth), Roger, Kenneth, Patricia, Mr and Mrs James Henry, Anne (wife of Roger), Kathleen and Henry.

The Diamond Wedding Celebration of Mr and Mrs Charles Sprague, held on 31 July 1969 at the home of Mr Noel Thomas. Standing (L-R) MrsVera Trinder, Miss Reba Thomas, Mrs Sally Pulham, Mrs Freda Davis, Mrs Edith Haines, Alec Hyett, Miss Mary Western, the Rev. C. Norton Tyzack, Mrs Maud Hanks, Miss Grace Collins, Mrs Elsie Wall, Mrs Lilian Lewis, Norman Auld, Mrs Tyzack, Mrs Kathleen Bartholomew, Mrs Hilary Quick, Jack Bartholomew, John Hopkins. Seated: Mrs Margaret Thomas, Noel Thomas, Mrs Sally Sprague, Charles Sprague, Hubert Yeates, Mrs Yeates. In front, Miss Jill Price.

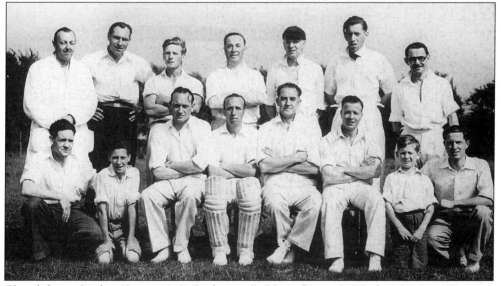

Churchdown Cricket Team, 1947. Back row (L-R) A. Dunn, J. Weekes, Mervyn Western, Hubert Yeates, Jack Lapham, Chris Moulder-Hill, R. Adams. Front row (L-R) Don Merrett and son, Charles White, Ken Sleep, Archie Packer (Captain), Des Shurmer, Charles White's son and John Yeates.

Churchdown Special Constables. Back row (L-R) Hubert Yeates, Bill Watts, -?-, Len Brown, Charlie Little, -?-. Front row (middle two) Reg. Merrett and P.C. Winstone.

Mr Leonard Brown, stationmaster from 1945 to 1957. He served on the Parish Council, was a member of the Churchdown Players and was also a Trustee of both the Richard Holford and Giles Cox Trusts. He is shown holding a 5th-century Roman oil lamp found in the garden of his home in Brookfield Road.

Mr Arnold A.G. Whitehouse, science master at the Crypt School in Gloucester from 1908 until his retirement in 1941. He celebrated his 100th birthday on 8 April 1978 (and his 65th wedding anniversary two days later.) He lived at Caledonia in Station Road from the time of his marriage in 1913.

The fascination of steam, 1961. Two young train-spotters near the station.

Acknowledgements

We wish to say how much we appreciate all the help we have received in assembling this collection, and thank especially the following for giving us information and so kindly lending photographs:

G.D. Bacon, Miss Lillian Bell, S. Blencowe, G/Capt. and Mrs A. Boden, Mrs D. Bridges, K.S. Browning, Mrs Betty Brunsdon, Mrs Dorothy Chambers, Mrs Clark, Miss Mary Colville, Mrs W Constable, Mrs Muriel Cousins, Mrs P. Coward, Mrs Doreen Cratchley, Mr and Mrs J. Dancey, Mrs Una Davies, L.F. Dean, Mrs Elsie Dodds, A. Done, Miss Barbara Drake, A. Garness, The Rev. Eric Giles, Mr and Mrs David Goodman, Mrs Maud Hanks, Miss Joan Holford, A. Hurran, Mr and Mrs Owen Hyett, Mrs Joyce Johnson, P. Lowe, Mrs L. Merrett, Mrs Rita Miles, Wing Commdr N. Neal, Mrs S. Nicholls, Mrs Hermione Oram, Mrs. Alison Pexton, W.H. Phillips, J. Positive, Mrs Dorothy Rawden, Mr and Mrs Sid Richings, Mrs B. Robinson, Miss Eileen Stamp, Mrs T.D.Stamp, Mrs B. Scotford, Mr and Mrs B. Smith, C.H. Smith, D. Strange, Mrs Margaret Thomas, H. Western, R. Western, Miss L.C. Vallender, M.J. Yeates;

and also: The British Legion, Churchdown Women's Institute, Gloucester and Churchdown Public Libraries, Gloucestershire Record Office, *The Railway Gazette*.

We gratefully acknowledge permission to use copyright material by: Russell Adams, B. Ashworth, *Western Daily Press*, Cheltenham Newspaper Co. Ltd, Gloucestershire Newspapers, Ltd.